TO: Wes M· · · · ·
The E
come
Dr. B. W. McClendon

MW00941535

Marriage is Not for Children

Dr. B. W. McClendon

3/1/15

Research Editor
Valarie B. Fleming

Cover Art created by
Crystal Whalon

CONTENTS

Forward

My target audience, of course, is men because God has called us to be the *Prophet*, *Priest*, *Protector* and the *Provider* of our families. The reality is that many of us grew up in a home where there wasn't a man, and/or especially a Godly man, present. In relation to being a Godly husband and father we had either no role model or very poor role models to follow. My heart goes out to so many men who want to be a great husband and father, but just don't know how. Information such as this would have been a great blessing for me and my wife in the formative years of our marriage, and could have saved us many nights, weeks and years of total frustration.

Regardless of your marital status, I challenge every man to read this book. Every wife and woman should put a copy of this book in the hand of every man that's in her life, and pray they would allow the Holy Spirit to do His perfect work.

Chapter 1

What is Marriage?

If the family is the building block of society, marriage is the quarry from which the rock comes. Marriage is not a one-time event; that is the wedding. To understand more fully what a marriage is, one must have a clear picture of the marriage process. Dr. Fritze states:

> "Marriage is an emotional relationship that exists between a man and a woman. This emotion is love. This is the essence of marriage."[1]

Sadly, many couples often mistake a wedding for marriage. What is the

---

[1] Fritze, Julius A., *The Essence of Marriage*. Grand Rapids, Michigan: Zondervan Publishing House, 1969, 23.

difference between a wedding and marriage? A wedding is the public declaration of marriage, and the start of a long and glorious journey of marriage. Herbert Anderson and Robert C. Fite, in their book entitled "Becoming Married," state:

> "The wedding is rather a commitment that two people make to each other in the company of family and friends and community and in the presence of God that enhances the process of becoming married."[2]

The wedding serves a dual role. It properly signals the end of courtship and announces the start of a completely new life

---

[2] Anderson, Herbert, and Robert Cotton Fite. *Becoming Married*. 1st ed. Louisville, KY: Westminster/John Knox Press, 1993, 2.

together. The wedding is the beginning of the *leaving* and *cleaving* as stated in Genesis 2:24, "Therefore shall a man leave his father and his mother, and shall cleave unto his wife: and they shall be one flesh." A wedding may be public or private but the meaning remains the same. It is the public pronouncement of a man and woman as husband and wife, and it is an indicator of their intentions.

Marriage is only for those who are emotionally mature enough to make this kind of commitment. A report from The Centers for Disease Control and Prevention in 2001 found that 48% of those who marry before 18 are likely to divorce within ten years, compared to 24% of those who marry after age 25.[3]The divorce rate for teenage

---

[3] Bramlett, Matthew D., and William D. Mosher. "First

marriage is high, because they are not emotionally mature enough to make clear decisions in their relationships. Research has shown that those who marry between the ages of 22-25 are less likely to divorce and have a higher quality marriage.[4] This is not to suggest that teenage marriages cannot survive, but it takes a lot of hard work. Speaking from personal experience, my wife and I were teenagers when we were first married. So from firsthand experience I know the challenges that confront teenage marriages.

Dr. Frize lists three components of marriage that are recognized by all fifty states. They are:

Marriage Dissolution, Divorce, and Remarriage: United States." *Advance Data* 323 (2001).

[4] Glenn, Norval D., Jeremy E. Uecker, and Robert W.B. Love. "Later First Marriage and Marital Success." *Social Science Research* 39, no. 5 (2010): 787-800.

"1) There must be mutual consent, freely given, on the part of the male and female; 2) Gaining consent of society to live together for the purpose of fulfilling a married relationship; 3) The last point is the physical consummation of the first two. This has a direct reference to a sexual relationship."[5]

Marriage cannot be forced! It is a willing declaration by a man and a woman. Society, because of the laws of Juris prudence, grants and gives permission for marriage, not the church. From the legal perspective, a couple has to obtain a license.

---

[5] Fritze, J.A. *The Essence of Marriage*. Grand Rapids, Michigan: Zondervan Publishing House, 1969, 22.

Society also determines what constitutes a marriage. However, the church and only the church has the power to bless or recognize a biblical marriage. In most states, society recognizes marriage as between a man and woman. Society does not recognize the following as marriages: 1) Children, 2) Homosexuals, and 3) Polygamy. The state is under horrific pressure from the homosexual community to recognize same sex marriages. Should this occur, because of the civil rights aspect of what you do for one you must do for all, the state would also have to recognize the marriage of adults with children and eventually polygamist.

Having conducted over 360 weddings, it is my belief that the success or failure of the marriage is set even before the wedding takes place. Two reasons have been noted.

First has to do with dating without a clear and definite goal in mind. The second is due to lack of premarital training. Let's take a closer look at dating. It has become a form of pleasure seeking, rather than an opportunity to get to know one's future mate. Dating should only take place within the context of courtship, which is the final stage prior to the wedding. Through proper courtship, a wedding date is set and preparation begins for the consummation of marriage. Dating without proper guidance can lead to premarital sex, which often leads to unwanted pregnancies, and the spread of sexually transmitted disease.

Dating, since World War I, has become a form of mate selection, which has no precedence in the Bible. Frank Cox states:

"Mate selections through dating is an American invention and is relatively new, having started after World War I, mainly because of the emancipation of women and the new mobility of the car. Some see dating as the most significant mechanism of mate selection in many centuries. In place of the church meeting, the application to the girls' father, the chaperoned evenings, modern youth meet at parties, make dates via telephone and go off alone in cars to spend evenings together."[6]

---

[6] Cox, Frank D. *Human Intimacy: Marriage, the Family and Its Meaning.* New York: West Publishing Company, 1982, 112.

Dating today, for the most part, is not for mate selections, it is to have fun with each other. Some think that they will get to know the person by dating them. There is a place for dating —it should be done within the context of courtship. As I have already stated, the date for the marriage has been set, so now the dating can really begin. Even within this context, the couple should not spend too much time together alone, because of the danger of premarital sex. Premarital sex is not the only danger, it can lead to unwanted pregnancy, which brings into the relationship an innocent person, who had nothing to do with the whole situation. Most of the time, in this situation, the man will leave it up to woman to make the decision whether to either keep or abort the child.

Consequently, regardless of what she does, she is still left alone and this is not right!

In Biblical times it was clear that most marriages were pre-arranged by the parents or there was a tremendous amount of parental or other adult involvement. One of the best Biblical examples of prearranged marriages would be the account of Isaac and Rebekah in Genesis chapter 24. In this notation, Abraham trusts his eldest servant Eliezer to go and find a wife for his son. His servant was instructed to go to his own country and find a mate. Apparently, it was love at first sight for Isaac and Rebekah. Not many are blessed that way. The problem with marriages today and why so many fail is because we are looking for someone to fall in love with rather than looking for someone to love. Consequently,

when the feeling is gone, the love is gone.
Love can only grow by being nurtured.

Previously, marriages involved a great
deal of parental involvement. An example of
great parental involvement in marriage is
found in the New Testament, namely the
marriage of Mary and Joseph in Matthew
1:18. (Now the birth of Jesus Christ was on
this wise: When as his mother Mary was
espoused to Joseph, before they came
together, she was found with child of the
Holy Ghost). As typical in the Jewish
tradition, there would have been great
parental involvement in the courtship,
engagement, and wedding of Mary and
Joseph. Similar, parental involvement was
seen in our culture for the silent generation
(those born between 1925 and 1945);
however, this involvement diminished with

the baby boomers (those born between 1946 until 1964). Largely, men left home for work or went off to school. In previous generations, they lived nearby and knew each other. Once the baby boomers left home, people did not know each other's families anymore. By the time most parents met the potential husband/wife of their children, the couple had already decided to get married without the benefit of knowing each other's family. Today, with the advent of technology, individuals from around the world meet and "fall in love", introducing even more cultural and geographic differences.

The lack of premarital training is another reason for possible marriage failure. We spend years in college and post-graduate work and less than a year to no premarital training. Hosea 4:6A, states: "My people are destroyed for lack of knowledge." In 2002, Dr. David Olson, author of the widely used evidence-based Premarital Personal and Relationship Evaluation (PREPARE) questionnaire and the PREPARE/ENRICH workshops, stated "that only about half of the couples getting married each year receive any premarital counseling (including what can be as little as one meeting with a pastor) which was up from about ten percent in 1992".[7] He contributes the rise to people becoming aware of the rising divorce rate and the desire to avoid becoming a statistic. The downside however, is that Dr. Olson

---

[7] Dr. David Olson, quoted in, Oliviero, Helena. *More Couples Get Premarital Counseling* May 28, 2002 [cited January 13, 2011]. Available from http://lists101.his.com/pipermail/smartmarriages/2002-May/001149.html.

estimates that only about 10-15% of couples actually receive any extensive premarital training.

In gathering my research, I conducted an informal survey in which the majority of the couples indicated that they knew each other less than two weeks before they got married. Personally speaking, the only advice I received before I got married was from my older brother. He told me, "Billy Wayne if you do what's right the Lord will bless you." Neither one of us were Christians at the time. That was the extent of my premarital training.

Premarital training is relatively new in the Black community; and generally speaking, it is not much better in the White community. Now we find that some state governments are getting involved in premarital training; example, in the state of Texas, couples are given pamphlets with information about marriage when they apply for a license. Some states give discounts on their license fees if the couple provides documentation of premarital training. Overall, there still exists very little premarital training, let alone the idea of marriage maintenance training.

Marriage training moves people from the idealistic stage of romantic life to the reality that having a successful marriage is hard work! In this stage of preparation, persons involved can discover whether or not they are ready for marriage. Through marriage training, they will discover that marriage is not a panacea and it will not solve all of their problems. They learn that marriage is giving and not getting. In their manual, "Before You Say "I Do", Dr. Wes Roberts and Dr. H. Norman Wright state:

> "You are probably about to begin one of the most important states of your life—marriage. Marriage contains unique and interesting potential. As one bright optimist put it, "Marriage is the only game in town where both players can either win or both lose"….We hope that you will have a much more realistic perception of yourself, your fiancée, and your marriage."[8]

The sad reality is that people will spend thousands of dollars on a wedding that will last no more than an hour. Yet they

---

[8] Wright, H. Norman, and Wes Roberts. *Before You Say "I Do": A Marriage Preparation Manual for Couples.* 2nd ed: Harvest House Publishers, 1997, 4.

want to spend less than $100.00 and ten hours to invest in their marriage. Something is seriously wrong with this picture. Marriage is like a building; if the foundation is bad, then the whole building will crumble. If there is not enough preparation for marriage and the storms of life come (and they will come), things will fall apart! Premarital training will help couples to identify those areas of potential conflict. The "Passage of Marriage" provides this information and inspiration to encourage couples to stay committed:

>"Not counting courtship, which by definition is a passage of pre-marriage, we divide the lifetime of a married couple into five distinct units. Although some people hasten

ahead of time into the next passage, or linger a little longer than average in one passage or another, in general, marriages hew pretty close to this outline. The passages are these: The first passage-- young love, the first two years; second passage -- realistic love, third through tenth years; third passage -- comfortable love, the eleventh through twenty-fifth years; fourth passage -- renewing love, the twenty-sixth through thirty-fifth years; and the fifth passage - transcendent love, thirty-six years and thereafter."[9]

---

[9] Minirth, Frank, Mary Alice Minirth, Brian Newman, and Deborah Newman. *Passages of Marriage: Five Growth Stages That Will Take Your Marriage to Greater Intimacy and*

Each of these passages presents different challenges for a couple. Without a spiritual foundation, there will be no stability to help sustain a marriage. Preparation is the big key for marital success and without it, the relationship will slowly die. Through these different changes for newlyweds, tremendous pressure is often placed upon the relationship. Since conflicts are inevitable, learning how to solve these conflicts should be a vital part of premarital training. Dr. John Gottman states in "Why Marriages Succeed or Fail":

"If there is one lesson I have learned from my years of research it is that a lasting marriage results from a couple's ability to

Fulfillment, Minirth Meier Clinic Series. Nashville, TN: Thomas Nelson Inc., 1991, 9.

resolve the conflicts that are inevitable in any relationship."[10]

Without this knowledge, marriages become stuck in anger, bitterness and un-forgiveness, which eventually leads to isolation and finally to divorce. Disagreements about finance, intimacy, blended families, in-laws, etc. are nothing but precipitating events and can be solved with proper training! Many believe that more states should follow the lead of Louisiana and require people to get several hours of premarital training before a marriage license is issued thereby giving the church greater power in its insistence as well. This would provide cohesiveness

---

[10] Gottman, John. *Why Marriages Succeed or Fail: And How You Can Make Yours Last.* New York: Simon & Schuster, 1995, 28.

between church and state in the regulation and performance of weddings. Since the wedding is another worship experience and celebration for the body of Christ, it is the author's belief that the state should only be responsible for the issuing of the license, and leave the ceremonial performance to the church. This provides opportunity for the fellowship of believers and a chance to witness for Christ, thus inviting people to become a party to the Kingdom of God.

"A Successful *Marriage*

Requires

Falling *Love*

many times,

always with the

Same Person."

Mignon McLaughlin

Chapter 2

Marriage is Christ Centered

This book is written from a Bible believing spirit-filled perspective. Since marriage is God's idea, people must be saved and filled with His spirit if they are going to experience what God had in mind when He created man and made woman. The creation account in Genesis is that everything God made was pronounced good. However, when God saw Adam alone in the Garden, God for the first time said, "It is not good that the man shall be alone, I will make a help-meet for him," (Genesis 2:18). Without the presence and the power of the Holy Spirit in the lives of both partners, the essence of marriage cannot be obtained. I am not saying that the unsaved cannot have a good marriage on the physical level; because there are a lot of men and women who are not saved and yet they have a fulfilling relationship in the physical. However, to experience and do what God requires, they must be saved!

At every wedding, you have the elements of a funeral. The unity candles symbolize two heterosexual adults coming together to form one single life. One's individuality is not lost; it is merged with another individual to form this unique and precious union. Consequently, both individuals must be mature enough to answer the call of their mate. The question must be raised; "what's best for the marriage", instead of "what is best for me or you?" Self-centeredness is the acid that

destroys the metal of romance! Without the
Holy Spirit, we cannot consistently live out
the demands of our marriage vows. The
Christian faith is the only one that starts with
presupposition that mankind is a sinner.
Reinhold Neibur talks about our
creaturelyness. The middle letter in sin is I,
and we all have "I" troubles. The Adamic
nature is the nature of a person wanting to
have their way no matter who it hurts along
the path to self-fulfillment. Racism, sexism,
elitism, divorce, etc. are all a part of the
Adamic nature. Paul talks about the fallen
nature of ours in Romans chapters seven and
eight, specifically in Romans 8:7, "Because
the carnal mind is enmity against God, for it
is not subject to the law of God, neither
indeed can be without the Spirit of God."

The carnal mind hates everything that is of God. This is the very reason why Paul warns believers not to marry unbelievers. (II Cor. 6:14-18).

> "Be ye not unequally yoked together with unbelievers: for what fellowship hath righteousness with unrighteousness? and what communion hath light with darkness? And what concord hath Christ with Belial? or what part hath he that believeth with an infidel? And what agreement hath the temple of God with idols? for ye are the temple of the living God; as God hath said, I will dwell in them, and walk in them; and I will be

their God, and they shall be my people. Wherefore come out from among them, and be ye separate, saith the Lord, and touch not the unclean thing; and I will receive you. And will be a Father unto you, and ye shall be my sons and daughters, saith the Lord Almighty..."

Many have violated God's law and have lived a life of misery and shame as a consequence of disobeying God's word.

If a man is not saved then he is not willing to take on the responsibility as a loving leader for his wife and family. The scripture teaches that God holds men primarily responsible for the life of the marriage. Men, by nature, are initiators and women are responders. I really believe that if I had not sought out and spoken to my wife at a football game in October 1970, we would have never met and married.

Solomon says in Proverbs 18:22, "Whoso findeth a wife findeth a good thing, and obtaineth favour of the LORD." The man does the pursuing before marriage and that pursuit is to be in a Godly way; consequently giving the woman the power of selection. God balances the call for women to submit to their husbands, by giving them this power. The woman then selects to whom she is going to submit too. I teach women to not marry a man they do not respect and cannot submit too. For the saved man, marriage becomes his ministry. He understands that the way he treats his wife is an act of worship. Karl Barth said,

"When marriage is seen in the light of the divine command, it is surely evident that the decision for the way of marriage is for some, as the choice of the unmarried state for others, the matter of a supremely particular diving vocation."[11]

Thus, as I minister to my wife I am ministering to God! Therefore, women who are married to spirit-filled men do not have to worry about being abused or abandoned. This will eliminate the idea that a husband sees his wife as a second-class citizen. This is how many feminist groups see marriage,

---

[11] Barth, Karl. *On Marriage*. Philadelphia: Fortress Press, 1968, 7.

which is far from the truth. There are those like Rosemary R. Ruether who says,

> "In orthodox Christianity, the possibility of a skepticism as a means of spiritual equality of women was suppressed in favor of the doctrine of patriarchy as the nonnative order of history. Women's capacities for spiritual equality are postponed until they reach heaven and are to be earned only by the strictest subjugation to male power in Christ and society. Late medieval culture thus, moves forward an increasing bifurcation of the image of woman. Spiritual femininity, symbolized by the Virgin

Mary, becomes increasingly out of the reach of ordinary women. Women, even nuns, are seen primarily as sexual dangers to men, carrying in their physical being the unrest of a debased subjugation to corruptibility and death."[12]

I would say to Ms. Ruether that these are some very strong assertions about men and the Church concerning women. It seems as if she believes that all men are against women. The *spirit-filled* man knows that marriage was and is for the protection of women and to bring forth the next generation. The National Organization of

---

[12] Ruether, Rosemary Radford. *Sexism and God-Talk: Toward a Feminist Theology*. Boston: Beacon Press, 1993, 80-81.

Women has called marriage, *legalized prostitution.* Sadly, so many women have such a misguided view of marriage. Unless one views the scriptures from a spiritual perspective, he or she could easily get such a distorted view.

The scripture Ephesians 5:22-24 (22; Wives, submit yourselves unto your own husbands, as unto the Lord. 23; For the husband is the head of the wife, even as Christ is the head of the church; and he is the savior of the body. 24; Therefore as the church is subject unto Christ, so let the wives be to their own husbands in everything.) is one of those passages, if not read in the *spirit,* could easily be misinterpreted. One of the big dangers in Biblical theory and interpretation (i.e., hermeneutics) is not reading the entire passage, chapter, or book in the Bible. Chapter five of Ephesians deals with the new life of the believer in Christ. Paul is saying that we are to be imitators of Christ as dear children. This new life is reflected in how we get along in society as a whole. We now possess the power of the Holy Spirit in our lives. The empowerment of the Holy Spirit helps us to live out the new life in Jesus. The main area where the new life should be evident is in our domestic affairs. Thus, Paul speaks to women first. The Greek word Paul uses for submit is a military word *hupotasso*, which means a yielding to another. This has nothing to do with superiority or inferiority. If a husband loves his wife as Christ loved the church, she need not be afraid to submit to and reverence her husband. For the spirit-filled husband, Christ is our example of a loving leadership. Thus, the greatest responsibility is placed upon the husband. Just as Christ laid down His life for the church, we must be prepared to do the same for our wives. A wife should not fear being taken advantage of when her husband loves her as Christ loved the church. This provides balance.

"Marriage is the only <u>Game</u> in town where both persons win or lose."

Unknown

Chapter 3
Marriage is Committed Love

Love has been so romanticized by the media and Hollywood to the point that even many Christians do not know what real love looks like. True love comes from God. I John 4:8 states: "He that loveth not knoweth not God; for God is love." True love is more than a funny feeling; it is an act of the will. The Greek word for love is *agape*, which has nothing to do with feelings and emotions. In I Corinthians 13, Paul gives us the definition and description of love and he drives the point home in verse 13, "And now these three remain: faith, hope and love. But the greatest of these is love."[13] As

_____

Christians, we receive love from the Father, which makes it easy to share this kind of love with our spouses. Jesus tells us more of what love does in John 3:16, "For God so loved the world that he gave his only begotten Son, that whosoever believeth in him should not perish, but have everlasting life".

Love gives without looking or expecting anything in return; therefore, committed love becomes the backdrop for permanence in marriage. Committed love is the glue that holds a marriage together as the marriage passes through the stormy seas of life. Those of us who have been married for a long time know from experience how crises can and will come into our lives, and can potentially wreck and destroy a marriage if both are not committed to each other in love. On January 23, 1998, my wife and I experienced the horror of losing a child! Our youngest daughter was killed in an automobile crash. The stress put on our marriage by this tragedy was almost too much for it to bear. But because of our commitment to Christ and then to each other our marriage survived and thrived. Praise God!

One writer states the following,

"The religious significance of permanence is linked to the promise that God's love has no limits. If marriage is a sign of God's presence in human life, then it needs to embody the same kind of commitment to love without end that we understand is at the heart of

God. The promise that God's love forever liberates humankind from anxious worry about failing to live up to the conditions of that love. It is a gift freely given without conditions of behavior or time. When two people promise to love each other until death parts them, that promise of permanence creates an environment without conditions."[14]

Committed love is unconditional and totally accepting of one's spouse. Human love is always trying to change the other person. We often say, "I would love him/her more if

[14] Anderson, Herbert, and Robert Cotton Fite. *Becoming Married*. 1st ed. Louisville, KY: Westminster/John Knox Press, 1993, 144.

only he/she would do this or that". Human love always finds fault in the other person. Human love is self-centered, but agape love is other-person centered. As Christians, everything that we do is motivated by our love for God.

Being married is agape love, a verb that is to be demonstrated during hard times as well as good times. I have counseled couples that have experienced hard times because of not demonstrating agape love. One example comes to mind of couples who have come to me after experiencing the loss of a child. The woman responds to the situation with much more lingering sympathy. Women grieve in a more profoundly different way than we men do; perhaps more because her life revolves around rearing children. If the man responds with insensitivity or with a lack of love, then the marriage will not survive.

Agape love demands that self-dies. There cannot be real committed love as long as self is on the throne. Self-denial is imperative if this level of love and commitment will ever be reached. The words Jesus spoke in Luke 9:23 (KJV) tells us that directly, "And Jesus said to them all, 'If any man will come after me, let him deny himself and take up his cross daily, and follow me'." When applied to marriage, these words become the banner of committed love. Because of our sin nature, we cannot love anyone but ourselves. The middle letter in the word sin is "I". Without the spirit of the living God in us, we would not be able to love sacrificially and give ourselves totally, the way Jesus demonstrated His love for us on the cross. Jesus was committed all the way to the cross.

I say all the time, jokingly of course, when her hourglass figure turns into a full day, there must be committed love. When we men get what I call "chest-of-drawers", which is when our chest drops down into our drawers (underwear), there must be committed love!

The Holy Spirit is liquid love, Paul says in Ephesians 5:18 "And be not drunk with wine in which is excess, but filled with the Spirit." Agape love comes from our relationship with the Lord Jesus Christ. Without that relationship, there can be no real permanence in the marriage. Karl Barth calls marriage the great command.[15] There is

---

[15] Barth, Karl, Geoffrey William Bromiley, and Thomas

no better way of demonstrating our love for Christ than by living out the love for our mates in a tangible way! Our children, grandchildren, and the world need to see an example of that genuine love. Jesus says in John 13:35, "By this shall all men know that ye are my disciples, if ye have love one to another."

Recent data from the National Center for Health Statistics[16] indicates at least 43% of all first marriages will end in divorce. Among those who have been divorced, 75% will remarry, and 39% of those remarriages will end in divorce. Christianity is no

---

Forsyth Torrance. *Church Dogmatics: The Doctrine of Creation.* Vol. III: Continuum International Publishing Group, 1990, 184.

[16] Bramlett, M.D. and WD Mosher. *Cohabitation, Marriage, Divorce, and Remarriage in the United States.* National Center for Health Statistics. Vital Health Stat 23(22), 2002.

panacea for the divorce epidemic either. According to a recent USA Today article[17], Christians have a divorce rate of about 42%. Evangelical Christians who do not attend worship have a divorce rate of 60%, while those who attend services weekly have a divorce rate of 38%. What a sad reality for the Christian church. Oh how we need to walk in the Spirit!

The second type of love in the Bible is Philia, which is friendship love. It is not sexual in nature, though (in the right circumstance) it can lead to or complement Eros (i.e., physical love). Philia is the kind of bond seen in scripture between David and Jonathan. It is the kind of love talked about

---

[17] Banks, A. "Christians Question Divorce Rates of Faithful." *USA Today.* March 14, 2011.
http://www.usatoday.com/news/religion/2011-03-14-divorce-christians_N.htm#

by Jesus who said: "Greater love hath no man than this that a man lay down his life for his friends."[18] Phila is the embodiment of everything true and meaningful, which is what friendship represents.

This kind of love for a marriage is very essential because it gives a sense of cooperation. There are times when a couple needs just to hang out together as friends, and do some stuff together. Whether that stuff is bowling, running, shopping, etc., it does not matter. In other words, being together, in a very relaxed atmosphere, without trying to be husband and wife. Consequently, the lack of this Philia love could be the reason why the divorce rate among Christians keeps climbing. My

———————————————

advice to couples is to take a chill pill and become friends. As couples strive to be friends, a great burden can be lifted from the shoulders of matrimony.

The third kind of love is Eros. Eros is the desire to draw out all that is good, beautiful and true. It is motivated by need, and is often understood to refer primarily to sex, which is really only one part of it – albeit a significant part. Eros involves the emotional need to elicit physical love and affection from the one you love. In most contexts, this involves a romantic kind of love.

One survey said that less than 3% of marriage is spent in actual sexual intercourse. However, this 3% makes up 80% of the marriage. Sexual intimacy in a marriage is like rain for the earth; without it, the earth would slowly die. Such is the same for a marriage. Without sexual intimacy, a marriage would slowly die. Thus, we see the tremendous power and the need for sexual intimacy in marriage. When a couple comes to me having marital difficulties, eventually I ask them how is the temperature in the bedroom. If there is a chill factor of -10° below, then I know the marriage is in serious trouble. On the other hand, if it is a balmy 120°, then I know the marriage has a great chance to survive. Sex is not the cure-all for marriages in trouble, but it can be a giant step in the right direction. Throughout the Bible, God has plenty to say about sex and its purpose in a marriage. God has one book in the Bible, the Song of Solomon, which specifically deals with erotica. The Song of Solomon was banned during the

Middle Ages because some thought the writing was too explicit. Paul says in I Corinthians 7:5, "the only thing that is more important than sex in a marriage is fasting and prayer". The honeymoon should never end, and according to Dr. Charles Swindoll in his book, *Strike the Original Match*, "That is exactly as God would have it. Now, there is no word here where things began to deteriorate between them [Adam and Eve]. Their intimacy apparently did not cool off nor did their love life wane. When God struck the original match, there was a blessed, enjoyable warmth that continued throughout that union."[19]

---

[19] Swindoll, Charles R. *Strike the Original Match: When Life's Pressures Have Taken the Warmth out of Your Marriage*. Grand Rapids, MI.: Zondervan Pub. House, 1993, 87.

In Deuteronomy 24:4, Moses instructs a couple to have a year's honeymoon. That's God's way of saying go and get it on erotically!

"Love is seeking
to make
another person happy."

Unknown

Chapter 4

Marriage is Communication

Just as evangelism is the life-blood of true Christianity, communication is the life-blood of a marriage or any relationship. Regardless of the kind of relationship, communication is the key to its success. To communicate is more than just talking about something. Communication is "a process by which information is exchanged between individuals through a common system of symbols, signs, or behavior."[20] To communicate means "to convey knowledge or information about: to make known and to transmit information, thought or feeling so that it can be satisfactorily received or

---

[20] "Communication." In *Merriam-Webster's Collegiate(R) Dictionary*. Springfield: Merriam-Webster, 2004.

understood."[21] When thinking of marriage as a house, communication would not only be the foundation, but the walls, wiring, plumbing, etc. If Godly oneness in a marriage is to be maintained, there must be open and loving communication. Communication is God's way of keeping a couple connected so that they may experience true intimacy in marriage. James 1:19 gives the way to maintain this kind of communication, "Wherefore, my beloved brethren, let every man be swift to hear, slow to speak, and slow to wrath."

God is saying that we should listen more and talk less. He has provided us with two ears and one mouth for that expressed purpose. Where there is no communication,

---

[21] "Communicate." In *Merriam-Webster's Collegiate(R) Dictionary*. Springfield: Merriam-Webster, 2004.

the relationship soon deteriorates. Communication is the life and soul of a good marriage; however, many miss the mark. The real problem lies in the fact that most individuals do not know how to properly communicate with their mate. Conflicts are resolved through good communication allowing the marriage to continue to grow. Despite how much love exists between a husband and wife, conflicts are inevitable in marriage. However, it is how these conflicts are resolved that determines the success or failure of the marriage. There are six areas of conflict that seem to appear repeatedly. I am not suggesting that these are the only areas; however, these six areas have presented the greatest challenges for many couples. The six areas are: finances, intimacy, in-laws, stepchildren, ex-factors and religious differences. In the next chapter, I will deal with each one in detail. As we expound on these areas remember that communication is the key to work through each one.

Inevitably, all good communication must start in prayer. The cliché, "the family that prays together, stays together" is true. Only through good communication are agreements reached. Agreement is the power of life. The minor prophet, Amos states in 3:3, "Can two walk together, except they be agreed?" When couples pray together, they become more honest, trusting, forgiving and transparent. Cary & Pamela Rosewell Moore, in their book, "What Happens When Husbands & Wives Pray Together", state:

"Yet it matters little why we --
just one happy couple -- have

developed a prayer life together if there remains no compelling reasons for every Christian couple to do so. We suggest that several compelling reasons can be offered, which may be called convictions for daily prayer as couples. The order in which they are listed here is not important, but we think these, at least, are the mandates for daily prayer together: 1) The crying, crushing needs around us; 2) the weakened, threatened state of Christian marriage; 3) the desire to be obedient; 4) the promised blessing of God's presence when two pray together; 5) the joy and added grace that come in seeing God answer prayer; 6) the help prayer gives in resolving conflict; 7) the door prayer opens into intimacy; 8) the fellowship with God prayer creates."[22]

Before God can do something through us, He must do something to us. This takes place when we pray and seek the Lord. Praying together will keep a couple united as one. Karl Barth stated, "If a man or woman is not saved, they will not see the relevance in praying at all."[23] As we ask God to forgive us of our sins, it becomes much easier to forgive our mates and

---

[22] Moore, Carey, and Pamela Rosewell Moore. *What Happens When Husbands and Wives Pray Together?* Grand Rapids, MI: Revell, 1999, 48.

[23] Barth, Karl. *On Marriage.* Philadelphia: Fortress Press, 1968.

ourselves. When we pray, we invite the Lord to enter our world and it helps us to be more like him. It is the power and presence of the Holy Spirit that teaches us how to be that loving husband and submissive wife. It is impossible without prayer.

Dr. H. Norman Wright, in his discourse on marriage, "Communication: Key To Your Marriage", says: "The number one problem in marriages today is not sex, money, children, but lack of communication between husband and wife."[24] Different backgrounds and modes of socialization often create barriers between the husband and wife. If these barriers are to be replaced with bridges, then communication is the vehicle to bring it to pass. True communication with Christ and each other is

---

[24] Wright, H. Norman. *Communication: Key to Your Marriage*. Ventura, Ca. Regal Books, 1974, 248.

the key to marriage. The desire on the part of both partners to communicate must also be present. Men must be careful in this area because by nature we do not talk as much as our mates. One study said that a woman speaks about twice as many words per day, on the average, as her husband. Therefore, when he gets home from work, he has done most of his talking. He is ready to grab the newspaper, flop down on the couch, turn on the television and go into complete silence. On the other hand, his wife still has a lot of talking to do! Women generally complain about their husbands not talking to them. Because of this "non-communication", wives often feel shut out of their mates' lives. Consequently, the door is open for her to have an affair; not necessarily an affair with another man, but an affair with her children, her career, church, community, etc. or anything that will give her security and appreciation that she fails to receive from her mate. Dr. Wright further states:

> "When difficulties occur in marriage, communication is usually involved. It may be the actual problem, or it may be the holding tank into which other problems spill. There are numerous types of communication patterns which are counter-productive in the marital relationship and there are factors which hinder communication."[25]

---

[25] Wright, H. Norman. *Communication: Key to Your Marriage.* Ventura, Ca. Regal Books, 1974, 248.

Through counseling many couples, I have discovered that couples who have had premarital sex have a difficult time communicating. These Christian couples have not asked for forgiveness and healing, and as a result, there is no real honesty in their marriage. They are not open and honest with God. It is God's design for a husband and wife to get to know each other on this serious and sacred level. God blesses this act of marriage to insure the intimacy is needed to sustain this kind of relationship. From Genesis to Revelation the Bible teaches sexual intimacy within the marriage bond to be looked upon as a celebration! Solomon in the Song of Solomon 7:6-9 states, "Isn't it refreshing to know that our God created sexual intimacy and He wants us to enjoy what was created for married people."

Forget your past sexual experiences and live in the presence of His wonder with your mate!

The areas of finance, intimacy, in-laws, stepchildren, ex-factors and religious differences can really get out of hand, if couples do not know how to communicate adequately. One study suggests that at least 35-40% of all first divorces could be saved if people would only learn how to communicate properly. George Thorman, in the "Marriage Counseling Handbook" states:

> "Most couples who seek professional help in resolving difficulties in marriage indicate that they have trouble communicating. Some complain that 'we never talk' or

'we have nothing to talk about'."[26]

I have found that the main road for intimacy is good communication, and non-communication as the biggest hindrance to a great relationship. Through proper communication, couples can identify the main conflicts; then they can find a way to resolve them.

Pre-marital training is a definite prerequisite to consider for a successful marriage. During this training, the couple, with some spiritual guidance, can discuss and explore their ability to communicate. Their instructor should give good advice and training in conflict resolution. Dr. Sherrill Burwell relates a six-step model for conflict

---

[26] Thorman, George. *Marriage Counseling Handbook: A Guide to Practice*. Springfield, Ill.: C.C. Thomas Publisher, 1996, 9.

resolution in her article "Improving & Strengthening Black Male-Female Relationships". They are: 1) Pray & Establish the Process; 2) Check for Accuracy; 3) Share Feelings; 4) Offer Alternative Solutions; 5) Pray & Proceed; 6) Follow-up. Let us take a closer look at these steps for conflict resolution.

Step #1: Pray and Establish the Process

As a believer, whatever we do, it first must start with a prayer. We pray to seek God's guidance through the Holy Spirit in how to proceed. Prayer brings a husband and wife together in the spiritual realm and reminds them of the vows they have taken, "for better or worse." For some issues they might need to fast and pray for hours, days, weeks, etc. in order to hear God's voice. Praying together helps to see your mate as your brother or sister in Christ, not as your enemy. Consequently, after praying about the process, it is established. For instance, we are only going to discuss this issue Sunday afternoon following our worshipping together for one hour and one hour only! If you cannot agree on this, then go back and start praying again. You never move to step two without agreement in step one.

Step #2: Check for Accuracy

Make sure you and your mate have the correct facts when you start your discussion. Each one must identify the subject that they are going to discuss. Thus, if the subject is money, then what about money are we going to be discussing. Are we discussing making, saving, or spending, because each of these can have a variety of different subtopics.

This is so crucial that couples are on the same page in their deliberations. The first step is only about presenting the facts; you are not sharing your feelings which will be the next step. Keep in mind at any time you can go back to step one!

Step #3: Share Feelings

This is extremely critical in conflict resolution because your mate needs to know what you are feeling. This is the step where you put all of the cards on the table. There must be total transparency at this point. No one should hold back any feelings. Let me also say whatever is shared must be shared in love (Ephesians 4:15, but speaking the truth in love, may grow up into him in all things, which is the head, even Christ). The feelings shared should only be about the subject that the two of you are discussing, not about the entire marriage. This is where many people get caught up in their sharing, they share and share and keep on sharing. Ultimately, we need to be brief in our sharing.

Let me quickly add that this is just a feeling, and because you feel a certain way does not make it right. Some people feel as if their feelings are fact. Feelings are neither right nor wrong, they are feelings. An important word to men, generally we are not as open as our wives are. So my brothers, as awkward as it may seem, this is your chance to really make a difference in the life of your marriage. Pray and ask God to help you to be open with Him and then with your wife. Again, I say to you, do not hold back, share your feelings!

Step #4: Offer Alternative Solutions

The idea that it is my way or the highway must go. Big Mama said, "There is more than one way to skin a cat." Let this rule be evident in your discussion. We must be open first to the Holy Spirit and then to your mate. This is where we must be watchful about pride, because pride will hinder us from receiving a different solution from our mate. Proverbs 14:12 states, "There is a way which seemeth right unto a man, but the end thereof are the ways of death."[27] It does not matter how sensitive the issue is, we must be ready for compromise, and if there is no Biblical precedent on it, we must be ready to look at other solutions to the problem.

Step #5: Pray and Proceed

If you set an hour to discuss this issue, when the hour is up, stop. Do not continue on and on and on, stop! Pray again for any hurt feelings that may have surfaced during this time. This is also where there might be a need for forgiveness on the part of both people. Do not give the enemy the opportunity to start it all over again in your marriage. Ephesians 4:26-27, Be ye angry, and sin not: let not the sun go down upon your wrath: Neither give place to the devil.

Step #6: Follow-up

Whatever you have decided on, follow through with those plans. If you decided to seek both spiritual and professional help, be sure to follow through on it. Proverbs 24:6 says, "For by wise counsel thou shall make thy war: and in multitude of counselors there is safety."[28]

Remember any time you are in doubt as to what to do, go back to number one!

"Patience is the ability to count down before blasting off"

Unknown

Chapter 5

Marriage is Reaching Consensus

In the previous chapter, I mentioned that many couples have their primary relationship difficulties surrounding six main areas. Those areas are: finances, intimacy, in-laws, stepchildren, ex-factors and religious differences. We will now take a closer look at each of these six areas in which couples need to be able to come to an agreement. You will notice that this chapter is longer than any of the other chapters in this book. I find this information critically important and that is why I spend a lot of time going over each area in great detail. The chapter defines marriage as "consensus" and consensus is just that – agreement.

Remember, agreement is the power of life. There should be nothing done without an agreement between the husband and wife.

Finances

To live in our capitalistic society we need money to get the basic things of life. One could exist without money, but it would be a very miserable and unstable life. The New Testament records that Jesus spoke more about money than he did about heaven or hell! Money in-and-of itself is neither good nor bad. It is your attitude and how you get, spend and treat money. The Apostle Paul in I Timothy 6:6-10 states: "But godliness with contentment is great gain. For we brought nothing into this world, and it is certain we can carry nothing out. And having food and raiment let us be therewith content. But they will be rich fall into temptation and a snare, and into many foolish and hurtful lusts, which drown men in destruction and perdition. For the love of money is the root of all evil: which while some coveted after, they have erred from the faith, and pierced themselves through with many sorrows."

Emile Henry Gauvreau once said, " I was part of that strange race of people aptly described as spending their lives doing things they detest, to make money they don't want, to buy things they don't need, to impress people they dislike." If couples spent more time focusing on pleasing Christ instead of other people, many of our marital problems related to finances would not exist. Roger Gibson said, "Unresolved arguments kill more marriages than any other problem.

What do couples argue about most? Money!"[29]

Both our spiritual and marital victories are tied into how well we manage our money. I was surprised to learn that 85% of all divorces are caused because of money problems. Solomon states in Ecclesiastes 10:19 (KJV), "A feast is made for laughter, and wine maketh merry: but money answereth all things."

My advice to all newlyweds is to stay out of debt, no matter what. There is great temptation to get overnight what it has taken parents 20 to 40 years to accumulate. I believe that these following steps should be taken and an agreement reached before they are married. If no agreement can be reached

---

[29] Gibson, Roger C. *First Comes Love, Then comes Money: Easy Steps to Resolving the #1 Conflict in Marriage.* Green Forest, AR: New Leaf Press, 1998, 11.

I strongly suggest postponing the wedding until one is reached in these areas. Remember, agreement is the power of life!

> 1) Make an agreement to stay out of debt!
>
> 2) Set up and live within a budget!
>
> 3) Decide if the wife will work outside the home and if so, how long?
>
> 4) Plan the number of children!

Next, I would give them a short practical list of things to do. I am not an accountant so this list will be very brief.

> 1) Pay your Tithes. God will not bless you the way he wants to if you do not obey His command to tithe. A tithe is 10% of your income. When the

question "do I tithe from my net or my gross, is asked? I simply say do you want a net or gross blessing.

2) Pay yourself; create a savings account with three to six months' salary. This is an emergency fund in the event you lose your job. Start your own personal retirement account as well. Look for safe, reasonable and sound investments.

3) Pay your bills. This is very important as well, because as Christians, it is a very powerful testimony. Isn't it sad to see Christians not paying their bills

or having insufficient checks
bouncing around town?

The above advice is a great place to start, however for more help, seek someone in money management. My recommendation is for every couple to take the Dave Ramsey Financial Peace Seminar. A great investment in the success of your marriage is the handling of your money! Financial freedom is next to salvation.

Intimacy

Because of the differences in men and women, intimacy can be another area of potential conflict in a marriage. For instance, when most men hear the word intimacy their first thought is sexual intercourse. On the other hand, the majority of women are thinking non-sexual intimacy, such as, a back rub, cooking, talking, and watching a movie, cuddling, going for a walk, or just simply being together. The big challenge in this area is how to recognize his great drive for sexual release with her desire and need for affection. Let me add, women are much more aware of their husbands' needs, than a husband is aware of his wife needs. This is what Peter says in I Peter 3:7: "Likewise, ye husbands, dwell with them according to knowledge, giving honor unto the wife, as unto the weaker vessel, and as being heirs together of the grace of life; that your prayers be not hindered."

I teach men that after marriage, they enter the universities of their wives. It is a life long journey of learning and discovering. I have entered my 43rd year of study, and praise God my GPA is steady rising. I have had some good days and I have had some hills to climb. I am learning how to be a Godly husband through the power of the Holy Spirit.

Wives, this is an area where you can be considerably helpful in instructing your husband as to what your needs are, (we are not mind readers). I call this the *McDonald Motif*. Whenever I go to McDonald's the person behind the counter always asks, "May I help you sir?" Even though, I look like I have been to McDonald's before, it is never assumed they know what I want. I tell them exactly what I want. Remember wives, following this simple advice could help stop many arguments about intimacy and sexual intercourse.

Men have the sexual drive and the women have the power of sex! In Genesis 1:28 God gave Adam the command to be fruitful and multiply. This sexual drive is for procreation and for pleasure. Because this drive is so dominant in the male, generally this can cause a lot of misunderstanding in the marriage. Dr. Tim & Beverly LaHaye in their book, "The Act of Marriage" state that a healthy man needs a sexual release every 42-78 hours[30]. This is a physical drive and is very real one. Without training in this area, the wife can begin to feel inadequate about satisfying her husband sexually. On the other hand, the husband can start thinking his wife does not want him. Moreover, for the husband, this can be the greatest form of disrespect. Without prayer and understanding the door could be open for an affair on the part of the husband. Sex is not

---

[30] LaHaye, Tim, and Beverly LaHaye. *The Act of Marriage.* 2nd ed. Grand Rapids, MI: Zondervan, 1998, 35.

intimacy, but sex is the fruit of intimacy. Sexual intimacy is the glue that helps to sustain and strengthen a marriage. The Bible is filled with example after example of marital intimacy. Lester Sumrall, in his book "60 Things God Said about Sex", states:

> "Our country needs to hear what God says about sex. He has not changed His moral standards to suite a profligate generation. He has not changed His plan for men and women to find sexual happiness in marriage. God's word includes an amazing abundance of information about sex. Nearly every book mentions sex, either directly or indirectly."[31]

---

[31] Sumrall, Lester. *60 Things God Said About Sex*. New

It still fascinates me how many older Christians act as if they are ashamed or embarrassed about sex. I understand about the generational attitudes, however, I think that if more seniors were to speak about it, some of the other generations may think twice before engaging in sex before marriage. It's disheartening for me when the majority of couples I counsel for marital training are already living together! Not realizing this act of sin diminishes the chance of them getting married. However, I have found that if they do get married the divorce rate increases another 15 to 25%, because they violated the sacredness of the marriage covenant! I have discovered that without serious counseling and forgiveness,

---

Kensington, PA: Whitaker House, 1993, 9.

the wife has the tendency to use sex as a weapon of control in the marriage. If she is not happy or does not get what she wants, there is no sex. In over 40 years of pastoring and having counseled with hundreds of couples, I have only had about twelve wives tell me that they never refused their husbands sexually! Wow! It has become a power struggle for so many wives. However, many do not realize that it is a sin to say no to her husband without an agreement. Paul deals with this issue very plainly in 1 Corinthians 7:1-5. It is a marital duty to fulfill the needs of your mate. Paul says in essence that fasting and prayer are the only two things more important than sex! Yet, if we are not careful, the beauty of sex gets lost in all the foolishness. Dr. Ed & Gaye

Wheat, in their book "Intended for Pleasure", state:

> "Knowing and understanding what God says about any phase of life leads to wholeness in that area; nowhere is this more necessary than in the sexual realm, where negative attitudes have virtually destroyed marriage relationships."[32]

The bond established from the sexual act is impossible to break. It is only broken through death! The marriage is broken by divorce, but the bond established from the sexual act can never be broken! What an awesome reality in this wonderful area of

---

[32] Wheat, Ed, and Gaye Wheat. *Intended for Pleasure: Sex Technique and Sexual Fulfillment in Christian Marriage*. 3rd ed. Grand Rapids, MI: Fleming H.Revell, 1997, 13.

marriage. It is through the act of marriage that couples can and will stay close. Staying close is one of the great challenges in a marriage especially for those of us who have been married for over seven years. With the ever-increasing demands on marriage with work, children, church, recreation, etc. it is so easy to drift apart. Consequently, sex can be put on the back burner of the marriage many times with sad and serious results. Yet, I have discovered that many Christian women, even after marriage, feel guilty about sex with their mates. Again, I think this is more of a generational thing, but regardless it is sad. Perhaps this negative feeling is coming from some of the teaching in many churches about sex. For years, the Augustinian view about sex was taught. St. Augustine was one of the great theologians of the early church. He felt that sex was a sin, even within the context of marriage.

St. Augustine believed that the account of Adam and Eve's sin against God (Genesis 3) uses symbolic language that the "forbidden fruit" actually stands for sex. He thought that Eve conceived and bore children in pain (Genesis 3: 16) because sex is sinful and any kind of sexual activity brings pain. According to Augustine, human beings should ask God's forgiveness for even thinking about sex and abstain whenever possible. In fact, Augustine said men and women who want to be righteous in God's sight should live in celibacy (i.e. without any sexual contact); his adherence believed their leaders should live in church monasteries and convents, without even conversing with the opposite sex.[33]

This is great advice for singles, but this kind of thinking for married people borders on being sinful. However, I have counseled some women who have been influenced by this mindset, and many never experience the full intention of God about the sexual act. The pleasure of sex is to remind us how loving and caring God is. Again, let me state that marriage is God's idea and to have this

---

[33] Sumrall, Lester. 60 Things God Said About Sex. South Bend, IN: Lester Sumrall Evangelical Association, Inc. 1993, 13-14.

kind of misconception is truly missing the overall plan of God.

Edwin Cole, in his book "Communication, Sex & Money" states:

> "Sex is the highest physical act of love between two people to show their union in spirit, which is a covenant relationship."[34]

God wants us who are married to enjoy this sacred and spiritual act of marriage. It brings a man and his wife together on the physical level, just as prayer brings them together on the spiritual level. The physical sex act is a bond by which a couple fosters love. Without this expression of physical love, the marriage would eventually die. The sexual act for men and

---

[34] Cole, Edwin. *Communication, Sex, and Money*. 2nd ed. Southlake, TX: Watercolor Books, 2003, 87.

women functions to keep them close. This closeness is so vital to the marriage in helping to maintain a sense of companionship. It is from the sexual act that a couple starts and continues to develop this sense of companionship. One writer wrote that during the course of a marriage about 3% of the time is spent in the sex act. However, without that 3%, the marriage would never reach the full capacity that God had in mind. Remember, the sexual act is the rain needed to keeps the marriage alive! This is why God has set His protections around sexual intimacy because of its value to the survival of the marriage. Without this sanctity, there will never be any closeness and it is the closeness that leads to companionship. Dr. Dennis Rainey in his book, "Stopping the Natural Drift toward Isolation in Staying Close", stated:

> "The choices you make determine the oneness you enjoy. Isolation is Satan's chief strategy for destroying marriage."[35]

Men, before our wives can really open up to us sexually, they must feel connected to us. The way she is made does not permit her to be able to turn her emotions on and off as we can sexually. Men, please hear me when I tell you, it just will not work. I know what the Bible says about and the expectation of that wife sexually. However, we men must help our wives in their responding to us by staying

---

[35] Rainey, Dennis, and Barbara Rainey. *Staying Close: Stopping the Natural Drift toward Isolation in Marriage*. Nashville, TN: Thomas Nelson Publishers, 2003, 8.

MARRIAGE IS NOT FOR CHLDREN

close with them. I have spoken already about companionship, but let me reiterate this very important dynamic that many men do not understand. It is through the development of companionship that our wives will feel emotionally ready for sexual intercourse. Remember, generally women sexually are like coals on a grill, it takes them time to warm up. Generally we men are like a microwave we get hot really quick! I will talk more about this in a later chapter dealing with courtship! It is in the area of courtship where we can prepare our wives for the sexual experience.

In-laws

This is the next vital area where a couple needs to have an agreement. In-laws can and will become out-laws; creating all kinds of pressure on a young marriage. (Genesis

2:24, Therefore shall a man leave his father and his mother, and shall cleave unto his wife: and they shall be one flesh). This passage makes it clear that marriage entails a weighty decision. Because of marriage, a person establishes a new community, which becomes primarily for them and it changes all of their other relationships. The individual is no longer alone, but now has a life companion, and must be aware of the impact of all choice and behaviors of him or her. In-laws can be a source of trouble. In-laws cause 40% of the trouble in early marriages. When you get married, you are only sleeping with one person, but you are married to the whole family and history. This is why it is so important that before marriage people will get to know their future in-laws! It is too late after marriage to discover things about your in-laws you just cannot stand or they discover things they cannot stand about you! Either way it goes, that is a **problem**. When I counsel young people, if their parents or parent do not approve of their choice of a mate, then I advise them not to marry until (hopefully) this changes. Don't fool yourself into thinking that love conquers all, not so. However, I do believe that the man has a better chance at a successful marriage, if his parents approve of the woman he is going to marry, (especially his mother). We are the ones who are commanded to leave and cleave. If the man is happy, he has a much better chance of getting his parents to accept her than the other way around. This is why marriage is not for children!

Biblically, when I think of in-laws two different people come to mind. Those two people are Laban and Naomi. Laban was a father-in-law from hell, yet Naomi was the dream mother-in-law. In Genesis, we are introduced to Laban. Jacob's relationship with Laban was rocky from the start because both of them were treacherous. Jacob had tricked his brother Esau for his birthright, and now it was pay back with Laban. Remember, what goes around comes around. (Gal. 6:7 Be not deceived; God is not mocked: for whatsoever a man soweth, that shall he also reap). This is why people should learn as much as they can about their mate and their mates family before marriage. Consequently, when you marry, you are marrying a whole family history. If there are any potential problems, hopefully they can be discovered in pre-marital training.

Now, on the other hand, Ruth and Naomi are the perfect example of how in-laws should get along. In the book of Ruth, you will read how she loved and cleaved to her mother-in-law Naomi. Because of Naomi's love for Ruth, she followed her mother-in-law back to Bethlehem. And because of Ruth's love for Naomi, she was married to Boaz and became the great-grandmother of David. Consequently, she was in the lineage of our Lord and Savior Jesus Christ.

Surveys suggest the order of potential conflict, rank as follows: a) mother-in-law; b) sister-in-law; c) daughter-in-law; d) father-in-law; e) son-in-law. This is generally speaking, your situation could be very different.

When I counsel young couples, I tell them that a safe and sure way of maintaining marital harmony in dealing with difficult in-laws is to let each person handle their parents. If I try to handle my mother-in-law, this would add insult to injury. However, if there is a problem and my wife handles her mother, things will work out significantly better! Whatever the situation, at the end of the day family is still family. This is especially true in the early years of the marriage and if this principle is continuously applied things will work out much better!

Remember a very simple rule of thumb: everyone handles their side of the family. If you follow this rule, your marriage will be able to navigate the sometime very cloudy water of in-laws!

Stepchildren

This is another area of high potential conflict. The divorce rate goes up when you are stepping. Because of the tremendous adjustment for everyone, I counsel single mothers who have a child or children over the age of ten, to remain single until they finish high school and left the nest. In these situations, the children are already hurting and angry about the break-up of their family, and many times without warning, they are thrust into these new relationships with a total stranger. The stepparent must be extremely sensitive to the needs of that child. Tom & Adrienne Frydenger, in their book "The Blended Family", states:

"One wrong assumption - that blended families are like original nuclear families with just a few more people here and there - can be hazardous to your mental health. Blended families have a more complex family structure and extra problems which seem to descend from nowhere."[36]

This tough problem is only continuing to increase. Every day in America, 1,300 step-families are formed. Whether stepparents are residential or nonresidential, they have a difficult position in the remarried family. Because the parent-child bond predates the remarriage, the stepparent begins remarriage as an outsider.

---

[36] Frydenger, Tom, and Adrienne Frydenger. *The Blended Family*. Grand Rapids, MI: Chosen Books, 1984, 41.

There are two stages that the stepparent finds himself or herself in: (1) Fantasy Stage – the beginning stage of remarriage finds the biological parent hoping his or her new spouse will be a better parent than the previous spouse. The stepparent hopes to meet these expectations and be appreciated. (2) Immersion Stage- during this stage the stepparent starts to feels like an outsider. Feelings of jealousy, resentment, confusion and inadequacy may surface as the closeness of the biological parent-child relationship becomes more obvious to the stepparent. The biological parent must be careful not to form an unhealthy triangle with the child and keep the stepparent in the dark. During this stage, it becomes obvious that they view the child quite differently.

However, the main two areas of tension are care and discipline. When counseling stepparents, I inform them it is best to let the biological parent do the disciplining; especially in the beginning of the relationship, it just works best this way. The other bio-parent has nothing to say if the child's bio-parent did the disciplining. The stepparent disciplining is a no-win situation and puts added stress on a very young marriage. For these and other reason's Tom & Adrienne go on to state the following:

> "When you marry and form a nuclear family, you usually have one set of in-laws and one set of children. Marrying into a blended family, however, is

like jumping head first into chaos."[37]

Stepmothers have a bad rap! The little research that has been done on stepmother families is filled with many of the same problems found in the stepfather research. In general, investigations of stepmother families confirm that clinical reports suggest that stepmothers experience a great deal more stress, anxiety, depression and anger regarding their family life compared to mothers in other family structures.

Dr. Pasley, in her research, surprised me in one of her findings about stepmothers. She states,

> "Of all the step-relationships the step-mother-step-child is

---

[37] Frydenger, Tom, and Adrienne Frydenger. *The Blended Family*. Grand Rapids, MI: Chosen Books, 1984, 85.

more problematic."[38] Dr. Pasley went on to state that these situational problems could be greatly minimized if the biological father is involved with the household and childcare tasks. It has been a great enlightenment for me to know this. Dr. Pasley also stated:

"These studies suggest that children in stepmother families are at the greatest risk for poor adjustment, a finding that is supportive of the work prior to 1987."[39] The father is the main

---

[38] Pasley, Kay and Marilyn Ihinger-Tallman. Step parenting: Issues in Theory, Research, and Practice. Westport, CT: Praeger Publishers, 1994, 7.

[39] Pasley, Kay and Marilyn Ihinger-Tallman. Step parenting: Issues in Theory, Research, and Practice. Westport, CT: Praeger Publishers, 1994, 8.

stability of any relationship and even more so in a "stepping" relationship. The father is the bridge between the stepmother and those children. He sets the tone. From the start, the biological parent must take the lead and set all parameters. Having this as the expectation from the start will make the adjustment easier. The father should not play favorites. Also, not just step back and let the stepmother and child work it out among themselves, this is where chaos can occur, making it difficult to maintain harmony and civility.

This knowledge is necessary for any woman about to assume the role of stepmother. There are other factors which could affect this as well; however, single women might want to re-think marrying a man with children, especially if you do not have any children yourself. It is easy to see how the divorce rate would increase because of this very important variable in a marriage.

The dynamics of step-father-step-child relationships seem to differ, depending on whether the stepfather is also a biological father or not. Stepfathers who have biological children of their own seem to fare better in stepfamily households. They feel more companionship with their stepchildren. Perhaps men with children from previous relationships fare better in stepfamilies because they are often less inclined to take on a strong parenting role, especially early in the remarriage.

The best example of a stepfather in the Bible would be Joseph, the stepfather of

Jesus. From the biblical accounts Matthew
1:18-25:

>"Now the birth of Jesus Christ
>was on this wise: When as his
>mother Mary was espoused to
>Joseph, before they came
>together, she was found with
>child of the Holy Ghost. Then
>Joseph her husband, being a
>just man, and not willing to
>make her a public example, was
>minded to put her away
>privately. But while he thought
>on these things, behold, the
>angel of the Lord appeared unto
>him in a dream, saying, Joseph,
>thou son of David, fear not to
>take unto thee Mary thy wife:
>for that which is conceived in

her is of the Holy Ghost. And she shall bring forth a son, and thou shalt call his name JESUS: for he shall save his people from their sins. Now all this was done, that it might be fulfilled which was spoken of the Lord by the prophet, saying 'BEHOLD, A VIRGIN SHALL BE WITH CHILD, AND SHALL BRING FORTH A SON, AND THEY SHALL CALL HIS NAME EMAN'-UEL, which being interpreted is, God with us. Then Joseph being raised from sleep did as the angel of the Lord had bidden him, and took unto him his wife; And knew her not till she had brought forth her firstborn son: and he called his name JESUS."

I have had guys tell me that they wanted to marry a woman with a child or children. The reason was, they saw being a stepfather as a ministry and opportunity to be a blessing in a child's life. To each his own, but I sternly recommend to men who are considering marrying a woman with children, to really fast and really, really pray about this decision. He needs to make sure that he is ready for the potential drama that comes along with the stepfamily marriage.

The survey shows that stepmothers can be more problematic with the emotional development of the children. However, today there is very clear evidence that stepfathers are more violent. Dr. James. Q.

Wilson, in his book "The Marriage Problem", states the following and alarming information:

> "Earlier in this book we noted that the rate at which children are abused or killed is vastly higher when they live with step-fathers rather than their biological ones. To repeat;: pre-school children living with a step- father were forty times more likely than those living with their biological parents to become the victims of child abuse and seventy to one hundred times more likely to be murdered by the step-parent."[40]

---

[40] Wilson, James Q. *The Marriage Problem: How Our Culture Has Weakened Families*. New York: Harper Paperbacks, 2002, 169.

If you are a single mother contemplating marriage please pray and consider what you are about to do. Make sure you know the man you are about to marry so you trust him with your children. This is one reason why my mother never remarried after the death of my father. Single mothers', do not sacrifice your children on the altar of your lust! I know the toughest job in the world is that of a single mother. I observed my mother and the burdens she had to carry being alone. However, the consequences could have been much worse if my mother had married a man who was cold and cruel; our lives would have changed for the worse! Single mothers', you must ask the question, why am I doing this? Is this for me or is this for my child or children? What is best for my children? Can I trust this man with my children?

Single mothers', please pray and seek God's wisdom before you bring a man into the life of your children!

Finally, I have coined a new phrase called <u>double-stepping</u>! This is when both parties have primary custody of their children. Now the potential for problems has just doubled, and in some cases triple. I know that there are a lot of variables in this situation, especially the age of the children. However, the challenge remains the same in trying to make a cohesive unit out of persons who are not biologically related. Dr. Patricia L. Papernow in her book "Becoming a Stepfamily" states:

> "Stepfamilies must do conscientiously, deliberately,

and simultaneously what people in first-time marriages can do over time, with less conscious effort. Individual in a new stepfamily must struggle to put words to a host of new, often unexpected and disturbing experiences. They must share these awareness's across great gulfs dividing insider and outsider, step and biological, and child and adult perspectives."[41]

This calls for a lot of hard work in trying to make a marriage successful. Stepping, to me, is like the race issue in this country,

---

[41] Papernow, Patricia L. *Becoming a Stepfamily: Patterns of Development in Remarried Families*. 1st ed. San Francisco: Jossey-Bass, 1993, 62.

never really solved, it is always lying beneath the surface, ready for conflict. Consequently, this is the reality of all stepping and especially double-stepping!

Ex-factor

The next area where agreement is necessary is what I call the ex-factor. The ex-factor is appropriately named, because how you get along with your ex will determine the success of your present marriage. Many get married and have not totally gotten over their ex. What I mean is they still carry the feelings for them after the dust clears, especially in those cases where there was no abuse or infidelity. Again, I reflect back to the title of this work. "Marriage is not for Children". Many immature people jump and get divorced too soon, divorce is a termination of the legal, not the emotional. Many couples come to me struggling in their marriages and the real problem is that one of them is still in love with their ex. This has to be a miserable existence to be married to one person and your heart is somewhere else. Dr. Jim Smoke, in his book, "Growing through Divorce" states the following:

> "Divorce, unlike death, does not fully remove the former spouse from daily existence. Former spouses hover about the edges of a marriage dissolution and frequently wreak havoc with the other mate's life. Different reactions of the involved parties in a divorce often relate directly to the

causes that led to the divorce."[42]

Now to those where the hurt is so real you have thought about physically harming your ex. Many times, these kinds of feelings are swept under the rug with all the other trash from the previous marriage. So often, these feelings are never resolved and this kind of negativity is passed on to the new unsuspecting spouse. Don and LaDean Houck have an excellent book on the is subject entitled, "The Ex Factor", they state,

>"Learning to deal with an ex-
>mate effectively is a problem
>all divorced people must face.
>Exes factor in every facet of am
>lives, whether we want them to

---

[42] Smoke, Jim. *Growing Through Divorce*. Eugene, OR: Harvest House Publishers, 1995, 29.

or not, and especially when children are involved. Sometimes the situations we have to deal with regarding our exes seem impossible to live with or to revolve."[43]

The Houcks are really right on in what they said. This is why it is so very important to try and come to some kind of reconciliation with your ex before you remarry. Many times the frustration being felt is stemming from the unresolved negative stuff from the ex. Then there are some cases where you are dealing with more extreme circumstances like child-napping, abusive behavior and death threats, just to name a few. This is why I cannot say it

[43] Houck, Don, and LaDean Houck. *The Ex Factor: Dealing with Your Former Spouse*. Grand Rapids, MI: Fleming H. Revell Company, 1997, 11.

enough, if you are thinking about remarriage, I strongly recommend not to marry until these things are resolved and/or you are able to deal with them. It would not be fair to your perspective wife or husband to be brought into this kind of situation. The Houcks also state:

> "During our marriage to each other, we have experienced both harmony and discord with our exes. It has not been sugar and spice all the time, but with a lot of determination, the relationships have become workable. We haven't always achieved the results we wanted, but we have learned to live with limited expectations and the

satisfaction of acceptable arrangements."[44]

This is why the divorce rate continues to climb with second and third marriages, because of the number of people involved and there is no workable plan for maintaining some sense of harmony. Just imagine the shock of this situation for your spouse if they have never been married, and have no idea what they are about to enter. Your mate could be madly in love with you, but not enough to endure all of the distractions that come along with you.

Think with me for a moment. A man never married, marries a women who is divorced; she was married for ten years and

---

[44] Houck, Don, and LaDean Houck. *The Ex Factor: Dealing with Your Former Spouse*. Grand Rapids, MI: Fleming H. Revell Company, 1997, 12.

she has three children, which range in age from five years to nine years old; the nine and five year olds are boys. Just for the sake of it, the husband's name is Billy, his wife's name is Betty, her ex's name is Jerry; the children's names are Jerry, Jr., Stephanie and Robert. Billy now has to deal with Betty, Jerry, Sr., Jerry, Jr., Stephanie and Robert. Of course, by now Jerry, Sr. has remarried and her name is Mary. She has four children, two girls and two boys ranging from the age of four to eleven. The four and eleven year olds are both boys and the six and nine year olds are girls. Because Billy, married Betty, he now has a total of ten people who affect his life directly and/or indirectly. In addition, if Mary's ex was to remarry, this family would expand even more. With this many non-biologically related people, it is easy to see why conflicts are inevitable and the divorce rate for second and third marriages are higher than first marriages. The Houcks further state:

> "Whether we are dealing with the ex-mate of our new spouse or the new spouse of our ex-mate, we have entered the world of "ex-hood". Both of these persons are in the non-control area of our lives, although they can exert a strong influence on our families. Whenever our mates resent or are jealous of our contact with our exes, it contributes to a lack of household harmony and inhibits the mental and

emotional well-being of any children involved."[45]

This is why I suggest that everyone handle his or her sides of the exes. If Billy starts talking to Jerry about the kids without an agreement with Betty, an already volatile situation can erupt possibly into a violent confrontation. Consequently, this only hurts everybody involved, especially the children, who are innocent victims!

Religious Differences

The sixth area of potential conflict, is religious differences. I caution people not to marry outside of their religious perspective, because of certain challenges they will face. Those two challenging areas are: (1) Where

---

[45] Houck, Don, and LaDean Houck. *The Ex Factor: Dealing with Your Former Spouse.* Grand Rapids, MI: Fleming H. Revell Company, 1997, 108.

will they worship? (2) What will be the religious training of the children?

The Bible is very clear in this area. In the Old Testament, God warned the children of Israel through Moses not to intermarry with the heathen women; because God knew the influence of these women to turn the men's hearts away from Him. This was one of the great temptations of Israel, to do just that with regrettable consequences. In the book of I Kings 11: 3, we see another example:

> "But king Solomon loved many strange women, together with the daughter of Pharaoh, women of the Moabites, Ammonites, Edomites, Zidonians, and Hittites: Of the nations concerning which the

LORD said unto the children of Israel, Ye shall not go in to them, neither shall they come in unto you: for surely they will turn away your heart after their gods: Solomon clave unto these in love. And he had seven hundred wives, princesses, and three hundred concubines: and his wives turned away his heart."

The power of a woman! I can write an entire chapter on that topic.

However, contemporary research has additional information in terms of religious differences in marriages. Studies by Zimmerman and Cervantes inform us of the following:

1) Couples with different religious affiliations have fewer children as compared with those who marry within their own faith.

2) These children are less likely to finish high school than those whose parents are of the same faith.

3) Six out of every ten children of a Catholic-Protestant marriage end up rejecting all religions.

4) About half of the Catholic men who marry outside of their faith abandon their faith.

5) The divorce rate of the intermarried is higher than that of those who marry within their own faith.

6) The teenage arrest rates for the children of the intermarried are much higher than those of the children in families where both parents are of the same faith.

The impacts of these interreligious marriages are just astounding, to say the least. Referencing 1King 11:3 again, no wonder God said what He did to the children of Israel concerning this matter. Within the hundreds of marriage ceremonies I have conducted, only one has been interreligious, a Catholic and a Protestant.

However, in the New Testament, Paul is very explicit concerning whom not to marry. In II Corinthians 6:14-18, Paul says:

> "Be ye not unequally yoked together with unbelievers: for what fellowship hath righteousness? And what communion hath light with darkness? And what concord hath Christ with Be'-li-al? Or

what part hath he that believeth with an infidel? And what agreement hath the temple of God with idols? For ye are the temple of the living God; as God hath said, 'I WILL DWELL IN THEM, AND WALK IN THEM; AND I WILL BE THEIR GOD, AND THEY SHALL BE MY PEOPLE AND WILL BE A FATHER INTO YOU, AND YE SHALL BE MY SONS AND DAUGHTERS, saith the Lord Almighty.

If you are single, you are violating the scripture by dating and marrying an unsaved person! To carry out the duties written by Paul in Ephesians 5, for both the wife and the husband, they must have the Holy Spirit in their lives. Trepidations are brought on by unsaved people trying to interpret and live outside of these divine principles. As I said in chapter one, the unsaved can have a good marriage, but they cannot love unconditionally as the scripture requires us to do. Paul also addresses salvation of one spouse after marriage, but not the other in I Corinthians 7:10, "And unto the married I command, yet not I, but the Lord, Let not the wife depart from *her* husband"

All we have is the word of God. If we live by the word, we can expect the power of Christ in our lives. The Apostle Peter also addresses this very issue in I Peter 3: 1-7:

> "Wives, likewise, be
> submissive to your own
> husbands, that even if some do

not obey the word, they, without a word, may be won by the conduct of their wives, when they observe your chaste conduct accompanied by fear. Do not let your adornment be merely outward—arranging the hair, wearing gold, or putting on fine apparel— rather let it be the hidden person of the heart, with the incorruptible beauty of a gentle and quiet spirit, which is very precious in the sight of God. For in this manner, in former times, the holy women who trusted in God also adorned themselves, being submissive to their own husbands, as Sarah obeyed

Abraham, calling him lord,
whose daughters you are if you
do good and are not afraid with
any terror. Husbands, likewise,
dwell with them with
understanding, giving honor to
the wife, as to the weaker
vessel, and as being heirs
together of the grace of life,
that your prayers may not be
hindered."

Peter is saying, that the conduct of a saved
wife should promote the salvation of her
husband. As a Christian wife, this is an
awesome opportunity for the Kingdom of
God, to possibly lead your husband to a
saving knowledge in Jesus! What an
agonizing existence as a believer knowing

that your mate is on their way to hell! I
have discovered that generally the man has a
much easier time leading his wife to Christ
than vice-versa. Women are responders by
nature, men are initiators by nature.
Moreover, if that woman loves her husband,
she may not get saved, but she will follow
him to church. The non-Christian husband,
for the most part, will not even be a C.M.E.
attender, (Christmas, Mother's Day and
Easter). My heart aches for Godly women
who are burdened down. To add insult to
injury, if there is a son(s), when he becomes
of age, he will follow in the footsteps of the
father and not attend church

If you are saved for God's sake, do not
mess up your life by disobeying the word of
God and marry an unsaved person. I agree
with Dr. Andre Bustanoby in his book

"When Your Mate Is Not a Christian", states:

> "It's very important for Christians married to unbelievers to recognize that unhappiness and conflict in marriage may not be due to the fact that the mate is an unbeliever. Conflict often continues even after the mate becomes a Christian."[46]

However, because a person is a Christian, especially the man, these conflicts can and will be worked out. Reason being, he wants to please the Lord. The unsaved person has no desire to please the Lord because he only wants to please himself. The believer is walking in the spirit of God,

---

[46] Bustanoby, André. *When Your Mate Is Not a Christian.* Grand Rapids, MI.: Zondervan Pub. House, 1989, 17.

so he wants to please his Father. Every believer sees marriage as a ministry; as they minister to their spouse, it is a reflection of their relationship with Christ and it is a visible witness of the love of God to a sinful world. The saved man has been commanded by God to love his wife as Christ loved the church and gave Himself for it.   (Ephesians 5:25 "Husbands, love your wives, even as Christ also loved the church, and gave Himself for it ;). In addition, the saved man knows that if he fails to treat her right his prayers will be hindered (I Peter 3:7 "Likewise, ye husbands, dwell with them according to knowledge, giving honour unto the wife, as unto the weaker vessel, and as being heirs together of the grace of life; that your prayers be not hindered"). Every Christian man knows the power of prayer.

Prayer for a Christian is spiritual breathing. What physical breathing is to the physical body, so is prayer to the spiritual man. No Godly man wants his prayers hindered!

Finally, on this subject, Jo Berry in her book "Beloved Unbeliever" says that the church needs to start a ministry for Christian women married to unsaved men. One of the main reasons for this ministry is that the unequally yoked wives are spiritually isolated. Mrs. Berry says:

> "They need to learn the principles taught in regular Bible classes, but they also need instruction on how to apply them to their everyday lives. Sometimes they need to be without their women who have a "soul" identity with their

problems and concerns. Yet, very few churches do anything out of fellowship and individualized instruction for unequally yoked."[47]

Thanks Sister Berry, this has given me an idea. Perhaps the women at my church who are unequally yoked could benefit from this ministry. I know this must be very difficult for you. Let me say it again to anyone reading this book, if you are dating an unsaved man stop it now! You cannot say you have not been warned! He could be a great person, however if he is not saved you are setting yourself up for a lifetime of trouble. Just as you trusted God

---

[47] Berry, Jo. *Beloved Unbeliever: Loving Your Husband into the Faith.* Grand Rapids, Mich.: Zondervan Pub. House, 1981, 162.

for your salvation, you can also trust Him for a saved mate.

King Solomon, with all his wisdom, still had 700 wives and 300 concubines! In the book of I Kings it is recorded how these women turned Solomon's heart away from God in his old age. What a sad testimony about King Solomon and his great legacy. These kinds of interfaith marriages can be extremely damaging to the people involved. You do not have to bring up the tremendous impact is has on children. Dr. Albert Gordon, in his book, "Intermarriage" states:

"Marriage between persons of different faiths apparently weakens the ultimate religious beliefs of such persons. What such marriages may do to the religious beliefs of the children of these mixed marriages must be even more startling."

This shows the inherent danger of these interfaith marriages and the impact on the faith. This is why many clergy will not perform a wedding under these conditions. One clergy stated:

"It is better to turn such people down even though I may be certain they are very much in love than have them look upon me or the church as a tool to be used whenever one has a mind to. I represent a certain view of life. I am pledged to preserve that way in sincerity and truth. I cannot give it all up to satisfy these people while I destroy my own religion." (93)

Gordon, Albert. *Intermarriage: Interfaith, Interracial, Interethnic*. Boston: Becon Press, 1964, 91.

This mind set is consistent throughout most religious circles. The main reason in not marrying interfaith couples is the maintaining of the religion. Research also indicates that these marriages have an even higher divorce rate.

"Agreement is the power of life."

B. W. McClendon

Chapter 6

Forgiveness

Many marriages deal with one or more of the situations discussed in Chapter 5, but before you can move past them, there must be forgiveness. Alan Paton says, "There is a hard law. When an injury is done to us, we never recover until we forgive". Forgiveness is the first step toward freedom in our lives. To forgive does not mean to forget. To forgive means the absence of malice. If I had the chance to do to you what you did to me, I would not do it. To forgive means you stop trying to get even with your ex, you let it go! Because if you do not forgive you are destined to be just like the person you have not forgiven!

Wow, what an awesome reality and a wake-up call too many of you, who are holding on and nursing that bitterness. Un-forgiveness is the cancer of your spirit-man. You cannot walk in liberty and victory until you forgive. You become toxic in your spirit and it spreads to your mate, who does not know what is going on. The intimacy in your marriage suffers because of your unforgiving spirit. Your unsuspecting mate is treated badly because of your unforgiving spirit toward your ex. Do not bring up submission to a woman with an unforgiving spirit, all hell will break loose! The spirit of un-forgiveness is why it is so hard to resolve conflict in a marriage. There must be a willingness to forgive.

These six areas that I have discussed are all high conflict areas, therefore, forgiveness is a must. Mother Teresa said, People ask me what advice I have for a married couple struggling in their relationship, I always answer: "*pray* and *forgive.*"

Mother Teresa is right-on with her advice because this was the pattern of our Savior. The first prayer that Jesus prayed on the cross was "Father, forgive them for they know not what they do". (Luke 23:34). If our Savior did it for His enemies, those who were killing Him, surely as Christians we must follow His example. In addition, we cannot do this without the work of the Holy Spirit in our lives. Throughout the Bible, we are told to forgive. Jesus, in the Disciples' prayer, said in Luke 11:4 "And forgive us our sins; for we also forgive everyone that is indebted to us."

Forgiveness is not giving someone a free pass to keep hurting you. No, No, No; even though I forgive you, I still hold you accountable in this relationship. Do not take my kindness for weakness! There is a difference between weakness and meekness; weakness is physical impotence but, meekness is power under control. Just because I do not, does not mean I cannot. I chose to forgive you and move on. Consequently, the only way you can move on is through forgiveness. Forgiveness is a command from our Heavenly Father who has, for Christ's sake, forgiven us. Ephesians 4:32 states, "And be ye kind one to another, tenderhearted, forgiving one another, even as God for Christ's sake hath forgiven you". Forgiveness is an act of the spirit, not of the flesh. Because in my flesh I

want to get even with my mate, not forgive!
It is because of our sin nature that will hold
us back from forgiving. Dr. Jay E. Adams
states in his book "Solving Marriage
Problems",

> "Obviously, the basic cause is
> always sin. But sin manifests
> itself in two ways in erroneous
> concepts and in sinful attitudes
> or practices."[48]

Without the Holy Spirit, there will be
no forgiveness. Un-forgiveness kills the
oneness in a marriage. Oneness is the
opposite of isolation. Isolation is the start of
death in the marriage, which is divorce. Dr.
Johann C. Arnold in her book "Why
Forgive?" states:

---

[48] Adams, Jay Edward. *Solving Marriage Problems: Biblical Solutions for Christian Counselors*. Grand Rapids, MI: Ministry Resources Library, 1986, 11.

"Over many years of marriage counseling, I have seen again and again that unless a husband and wife forgive each other daily, marriage can become a living hell. I have also seen that the thorniest problems can often be resolved with three simple words: 'I am sorry'."[49]

If you are reading this book and you have un-forgiveness in your heart toward your mate, forgive them now and if you were wrong, ask your mate to forgive you. Dr. Arnold goes on to say:

"Asking one's partner for forgiveness is always difficult because it requires humility, vulnerability and the

---

[49] Arnold, Johann Christoph. *Why Forgive?* Rifton, NY: Plough Publishing House, 2009, 11.

acknowledgment of weakness and failure. Yet there are few things that make a marriage healthier."[50]

You may want to stop reading this book and ask the Lord to forgive you for holding your mate hostage through un-forgiveness. By doing this, you will release a spiritual freshness in your marriage that will just knock your socks off! Moreover, the honeymoon will never end. Now, if you were wronged then you must forgive your mate! Once this is done, you can really get on with your life and truly enjoy the freedom that only Christ can bring.

Finally, the first five areas that we have just finished looking at are highly volatile, if not handled properly. This is why

---

[50] pg. 117

there is a proliferation of domestic violence in our homes. Reports show that every fifteen seconds a woman in America is assaulted by her boyfriend or husband. Needless to say, this is too high and out of control. There are some women who are guilty, but overwhelmingly, it is most men who are guilty! Men, this is not how we show love to our wives! Get some help and do it now! The only we should put our hands on or wives is to caress them and love them as Christ loved the church. Women, if you are in an abusive marriage, get out now! If he hit you one time, he will hit you again. Therefore, I say it again, get out of this situation and do it now! If you are single and dating a man who exhibits some of these abusive tendencies, get out now. Some of you could have grown up in these abusive homes; however, this is not God's way.

Let's discuss conflict resolution, to help some of you who are struggling. Dr. John Gottman states in his book "Why Marriages Succeed or Fail":

> "If there is one lesson I have learned from my years of research it is a lasting marriage results from a couple's ability to resolve the conflicts that are inevitable in any relationship."[51]

The key that can and will turn and save your marriage is, conflict resolution. I agree wholeheartedly with Dr. Gottman that conflicts are inevitable in a marriage.

---

[51] Gottman, John Mordechai, and Nan Silver. *Why Marriages Succeed or Fail: _and How You Can Make Yours Last*. 1st ed. New York: A Fireside Book, 1995, 28.

However, if handled properly, they could strengthen the marriage in such a profound way. It is so very important that conflict resolution skills are learned and applied in each marriage. Men, since God holds us primarily responsible for the life of the marriage we should be leading the way in this area. Remember men, our wives respond to how they are treated. There are many books written on this subject. However, I like to take the simplest approach to resolving conflicts. Dr. Harrell C. Hines in his book "Resolving Conflict in Marriage"

> "God prepared the success of your marriage long before you ever got married. He set out the plan that would allow you to be happily, joyfully and

successfully married. Your part is to walk out God's plan. It's as you walk out His plan and not your own plan that your marriage takes on a deeper meaning and a deeper joy. It's then that marriage becomes truly satisfying and fulfilling."[52]

Step one in resolving conflict is to pray together. Spend time praying with each other and praying for each other. Prayer helps a couple to focus on the Lord Jesus Christ and their marriage, not on themselves. Remember, the goal of every believer is to please the Lord. This destroys all pettiness in a marriage. Step two: a couple needs to define the issue that they are going to discuss. This will cut out all rambling and

---

[52] Hines, Darrell. *Resolving Conflict in Marriage*. New Kensington, PA: Whitaker House, 2001, 11.

keep them on track. One reason why it is so hard to resolve issues is because this step is violated. If you are going to discuss money, then money is all that you should discuss. Make sure this step is clearly defined and understood that at this time we are only to be discussing money. Any attempt otherwise will sabotage the process. Then specify what area of money will be discussed, budgeting investments, life insurance, will, etc. Step three: set a time limit on how long you are going to discuss the topic. Too many couples mess up the whole week by not having a time set and a day to discuss those challenging topics. Some issues do not have a quick resolution. Those are the ones you might want to get help with from your pastor or some other professional. Remember the most important thing is maintaining the integrity of the marriage. Step four: make sure to forgive each other for any hurts that might have occurred. There is a great danger in letting un-forgiveness continue. Paul says in Ephesians 4:26-27, "Be ye angry and sin not; let not the sun go down upon your wrath; neither give place to the devil."

Step five: close with prayer and celebrate God's goodness in your marriage. Regardless of whether or not you solve the issue, spend the rest of the time talking about what you do agree on and celebrate that! Celebration can range from going for a walk together or having mad passionate sex! However you do it, Celebrate! Again, I say Celebrate! Again, I say Celebrate!

"He who cannot forgive breaks the bridge over which he himself must pass."

George Herbert

Chapter 7

Marriage is Courtship

Finally, I would like to look at the process of courtship. The word courtship means, "To engage in social activities leading to engagement and marriage." This is a very important step in the whole marriage encounter. My thoughts on courtship are as follows; there are two types, pre-marital and post-marital.

The first type is pre-marital courtship, which I call dating, which should take place only within the courtship stage. This may sound strange to many of you because of the sinful way we have been doing business in America. As I stated earlier, before World War II, dating was done for the sole purpose of mate selection. In other words, before a couple started dating, they knew they were going to be married. However, after World War II, dating was done more for pleasure. It was a man and woman going out together to have fun. No kind of commitment at all, it was strictly for fun. Consequently, around 1960 the birth control pill was invented making sex safer, because you had eliminated the fear of pregnancies. Thus, pre-marital sex became a part of this equation with all kinds of devastating results. Majority of people coming to see me for pre-marital and post-marital maintenance are having or have had pre-marital sex! Because the sex is good, many people feel and think they are in love; not realizing that pre-marital sex increases the likelihood of them not getting married. Every relationship runs on two very important tracks, which are trust and respect. Pre-marital sex destroys both of these tracks in a very profound way, especially for the man. On average, men will lose respect for the woman a lot faster than the woman for the man. In addition, the trust factor can be easily evaporated was well. Reason being, the average man thinks if you have sex with him while not being married to him, then you will have sex with other men. However, for the average woman, that's the last thing she has on her mind, having sexual intercourse with another man. This is one cause of the high divorce rate in this country. The sad reality of this is that the Christian church divorce rate is the same as the world, because Christians are participating in the same sin. This is the sin of fornication.

I have also discovered a high percentage of these cases women will use sex as a bargaining chip once they get married. Sex is used by the wife to control her husband, conflict means less sex for hubby. In 40 years of pastoring and counseling, only twelve wives have told me they have never refused their husbands sexually. This is really a shame, considering the high priority God places on sex and marriage. This kind of game playing could lead a man into some serious sexual situations, however, regardless of the situation; a man never has the right to be unfaithful to his wife. For some men an affair may not be with another woman, sometimes it could be pornography, which is dangerous within itself. You are doing more harm to the relationship than good and it increases the likelihood that you will not get married. Remember that women have the power of sex and we men have the sexual drive. It is much easier for women to say no to her boyfriend than the boyfriend to his girlfriend. Therefore, women, do not use your bodies to influence that man to marry you sooner than he wants to.

One final thought on this, non-marital sex is like driving and drinking, it will affect your perception. This is the cause of important issues being overlooked and put on the back burner to be dealt with after the wedding. Consequently, many of these issues are not worked out and they contribute to the death of the marriage, which is divorce. Remember, sex is a gift from God to married couples only to enjoy with each other! There should be no hand holding or kissing until after the wedding, because Jesus says in Matthew 26:41 "Watch and pray, that ye enter not into temptation; the spirit indeed is willing, but the flesh is weak." Moreover, if you cannot keep your hands off each other, then do what the Apostle Paul says in I Corinthians 7:9: "But if they cannot have self-control, let them marry, for it is better to marry than to bum." As a single Christian dating, make an agreement with your partner to marry immediately if you have sex. Get married or never be alone together again. You may ask do you get married just for the sex. No, however, as a believer you get married to honor God in your life and to be a witness to others about Jesus!

The second type of courtship is post-marital dating.   This is when time can become the potential killer of enthusiasm. In Genesis 26:8, there is a fascinating account of Isaac and Rebekah; it reads:

> "And it came to pass, when he had been there a long time, that Abimelech, King of the Philistines, looked out a window, and saw, and behold, Isaac was sporting with Rebekah, his wife.

Sporting is an old King James word which means caress. In other words, Isaac was caressing Rebekah who was not his sister. Remember, for fear of his life, Isaac had told Abimelech that Rebekah was his sister.

Men, this is where a lot of us fall very short, which I previously discussed in chapter 5 on intimacy, but let me reiterate this again. Our wives need and want our affection so very, very, very, very much! She still needs to know that she is the one. The sad reality for the most part is, because we men are conquerors once we get married after few years, we lose interest in our wives, except for the sex. The longer we are married, the more we need to court our wives. There are two main reasons why I feel this is so important. First, it boosts her confidence in herself. In our society, older married women are expendable, much more than men. In the American of African descent community, there is a plethora of available women compared to the number of men. Therefore, our wives need the constant assurance that they still have it and we would marry them all over again. My second reason ties into the first, we need to court our wives for security, the security in knowing that we are not going to dump them and marry a younger trophy wife. This is happening more and more every day! One of the biggest fears of many middle-aged women is being dumped by their husbands. When they see it happening to their friends you can be sure they are thinking that it could happen to them. Because of women and their closeness, it can be as if it has happened to them. I Peter 3:7 speaks to this:

"In like manner, ye husbands dwell with them according to knowledge, giving honor unto the wife, as unto the weaker vessel and as being heirs together of the grace of life, that your prayers be not hindered."

I teach men that when we get married we enter the University of our Wives, because women are more complex than we are. Once we learn about her and put it into practice, the fire of love will continue to burn. In other words, the honeymoon will never end. Charles Swindoll, in his book "Strike the Original Match" makes this same assertion. He states:

> "For starters, we need to redefine honeymoon. You're not going to like my suggestion: adjustment period…. But wait a minute, that's exactly what it is! It's the beginning of a whole new life-style. Sure, the honeymoon does include that initial burst of physical intimacy, that period of passionate ecstasy between the wedding ceremony and the

return to life's responsibilities.... If a couple begins this adjustment period with all four feet firmly fixed on reality, it's doubtful that they will suffer many sudden disappointments."[53]

I have been instructing young couples about this for years. I call it a major adjustment period. With all of the baggage that so many couples bring into their marriages, many do not even enjoy the honeymoon. In fact, many get married on Saturday and are back to work on Monday morning, back into the hustle and bustle of life. Many have been living together and have children from previous marriages or

---

[53] Swindoll, Charles R. *Strike the Original Match: When Life's Pressures Have Taken the Warmth out of Your Marriage.* Grand Rapids, MI.: Zondervan Pub. House, 1993, 85-86.

relationships and the money is already funny. This is a disaster just waiting to happen! Moses, in Deuteronomy 24:5 says:

> "When a man hath taken a new wife, he shall not go out to war, neither shall he be charged with any business, but he shall be free at home one year, and he shall cheer up his wife whom he hath taken."

In my years of pastoring, I have not met a couple who had a honeymoon that lasted for a year. The responsibility is placed on the husband to cheer up his wife. A great way to get started is to have 365 days to get to know each other without any distractions. It is in the first year that the foundation is laid for a successful marriage. Our wives respond to how we treat them, if we are loving and kind, that's what we will receive in return. Men we need to keep striking that match and putting good dry wood on the flames! Then we can rejoice in the warmth of her love.

Finally, I have discovered that one of the greatest killers of the post-marital courtship for many men is the lack of sexual intercourse with their wives. On the average, men have a higher sex drive for intercourse, which does not mean that women do not enjoy sex just as men do, but it is a known fact that women do not need sexual intercourse as often as men do. Drs. Tim & Beverly LaHaye in their book "The Act of Marriage" says, a healthy man needs to have a sexual release every 42-78 hours, this is biologically driven and not just in a man's head. It is part of God's divine plan for man to procreate as He has commanded. Men have the sexual drive and women have the power of sex. This is why if a man has sex with a woman against her will it is rape. In the hustle and bustle of life, how can a man and his wife have an agreement in this area? I have counseled many couples who have a great marriage, but this area is about to kill their relationship. Especially if there are children in the marriage and the wife works outside the home. It has been documented that a stay-at-home mom works very hard, but if she works outside the home, she is literally working 24/7. At the end of the day she is tired from all the ripping and running, and then about 10:00 pm her husband wants to have sex. She's exhausted with nothing left to give. If this continues to happen, the marriage could be in serious trouble and

possibly headed toward divorce. Sex is the
nurturing rain that keeps the marriage alive
and the marriage will grow and flourish. For
years, I have been suggesting to married
couples to schedule their sex time. I know
some of you are thinking that this is not
romantic. Isn't it funny how we schedule
everything else because of our busy agenda,
then why not sex, if this will help save your
marriage. Jill Savage, in her book "Is There
Really Sex after Kids?" states the following
reasons why scheduling sex can work
wonders for your marriage:

(l) Scheduling sex eliminates
"The Ask", (2) Scheduling sex
increases desire, (3) Scheduling
sex increases anticipation, (4)
Scheduling sex allows for
prime time planning, (5)

Scheduling sex helps couples prepare physically, (6) Scheduling sex builds trust in a marriage.

Perhaps you and your spouse need to ask God to forgive you, then ask each other for forgiveness. If you have hurt your mate with an unloving spirit, you might need to adjust your attitude about sex. Many married people have negative ideas about sex. Sex is God's gift to a married couple for 1) procreation, 2) pleasure. God wants us to enjoy sex as we enjoy his creation; the Bible is filled with passage after passage about sex. It is best summed as the blessing of monogamy and the curse of adultery. Let us keep our marriage strong for a witness to this dying world about Jesus and to leave a lasting legacy for our children, grandchildren, etc.

I pray and hope that this book has blessed and challenged you to reaffirm your vows and live them out together the way God intended. I challenge every man to be the Prophet, Priest, Protector and Provider of his family, and quoting my wife every woman should be her husbands, Crown, Completer, Companion and Confidant. If you are not saved, now is a good time to ask the Lord Jesus to come into your life. The Bible says in Romans 10:13 "For whosoever shall call upon the name of the Lord shall be saved."

If you ask Jesus to save you, then welcome to the family of God. Now, go join a Bible preaching and teaching church so you can grow in the knowledge and wisdom of God. Moreover, be sure to tell everyone you meet about this man called Jesus!

"A lot of people are lonely because they build walls instead of bridges."

Unknown

Acknowledgements

Giving praise and glory to my Lord and Savior Jesus Christ. Honor to my parents, the late Leroy and Leora McClendon. To my children, I express love and gratitude for your support to me as PK's. Now you are adults with your own families. I pray the legacy continues.

To my wife, who has been my number one supporter, thank you and I love you. I know without a doubt what I have accomplished could not have been done without you.

To the members of one of the greatest churches in the world, "St. James" thank you for 20 years of love and support.

Thank you to all who helped with this project in whatever way. I appreciate all of the work, time, prayers and support.

A special thank you to Dr. Valarie Fleming , Sis. Crystal Whalon of W Design Firm and Sis. Willie Odems.

Booking Contact

Thank you for your purchase of this book. For conference, seminar or bible study booking please contact *marriageisnotforkids@gmail.com*

Scripture References

All scripture reference was taken from the King James Version of the Bible public domain.

Now unto Him who is able to keep you from falling, and present you faultless before the presence of His glory with exceeding joy. To the wise God our Savior, be glory and majesty, dominion and power, both now and ever.

Amen

Jude 24-25

15143615R00102

Made in the USA
San Bernardino, CA
16 September 2014